HAL•LEONARD®

DRUM PLAY-ALONG™

AUDIO
ACCESS
INCLUDED

PLAYBACK+
Speed • Pitch • Balance • Loop

Hal•Leonard®

Top Rock Hits

Play 9 Songs with Sound-alike Audio

T0039562

To access audio visit:
www.halleonard.com/mylibrary

Enter Code
8229-6195-1112-3839

ISBN 978-1-5400-1532-7

HAL•LEONARD®

7777 W. BLUEMOUND RD. P.O. BOX 13819 MILWAUKEE, WI 53213

Visit Hal Leonard Online at
www.halleonard.com

CONTENTS

Page	Title
4	Believer IMAGINE DRAGONS
12	Can't Feel My Face THE WEEKND
9	Heathens TWENTY ONE PILOTS
16	Human RAG 'N' BONE MAN
19	Lonely Boy THE BLACK KEYS
22	My Songs Know What You Did in the Dark (Light Em Up) FALL OUT BOY
26	Paradise COLDPLAY
32	Unsteady X AMBASSADORS
35	Wish I Knew You THE REVIVALISTS

Believer

Words and Music by Dan Reynolds, Wayne Sermon, Ben McKee,
Daniel Platzman, Justin Trantor, Mattias Larsson and Robin Fredricksson

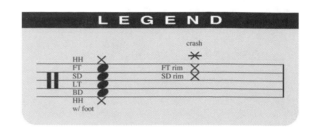

Intro
Moderate Rock ♩ = 125
Half-time feel

*Large tom (LT) positioned on left side and played with left stick.

Verse

1. First things first: I'm-a say all the words in-side my head. I'm fired up and
2. *See additional lyrics*

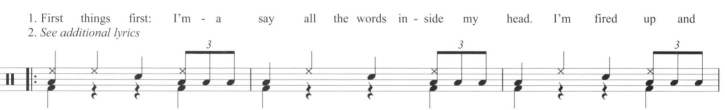

tired of the way that things have been, oh, ooh, _____ the way that things have

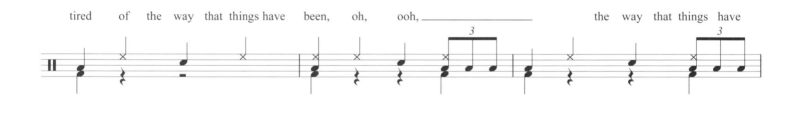

been, oh, ooh. _____ I was

Pre-Chorus

bro - ken _____ from a young age, tak-ing my sulk-ing _____ to the mass-es, writ-ing my

po - ems ____ for the few that looked at me, took to me, shook to me, feel - ing me sing - ing from

heart - ache, ___ from the pain, tak - ing my mes - sage ____ from the veins, speak - ing my

les - son ____ from the brain, see - ing the beau - ty _____ through the...

𝄋 Chorus

pain! You made me a, you made me a be - liev - er, be -

liev - er. Pain! You break me down, you build me up; be -

liev - er, be - liev - er. Pain! _____ Oh, let the bul - lets fly, oh, let them

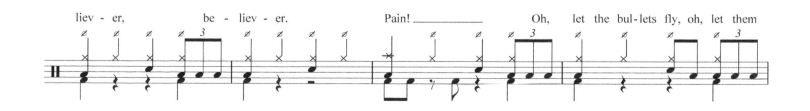

rain. _____ My life, my love, my drive, they came from... pain! You

To Coda ⊕

made me a, you made me a be - liev - er, be - liev - er.

Verse

3. Third things third: send a prayer to the ones ___ up a - bove. All the hate that you've

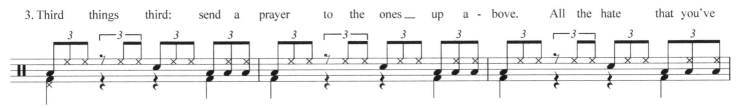

heard has turned your spir - it to a dove, oh, ooh, _____ your spir - it up a -

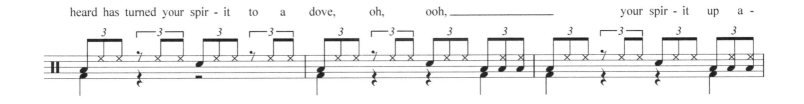

Pre-Chorus

bove, oh, ooh. _____ I was chok - ing ___ in the crowd, liv - ing my

brain up ___ in the cloud, fall - ing like ash - es ___ to the ground, hop - ing my

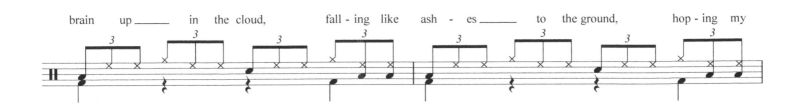

feel - ings, ___ they would drown.   But they nev - er did, ev - er lived, ebb - ing and flow - ing, in -

hib - it - ed, lim - it - ed, till it broke up and it rained down,   it rained ___

D.S. al Coda   **Coda**

down ___   like...   liev - er.

Verse

4. Last things last: by the grace of the fi - re and the flames, you're the face of the

fu - ture, the blood __ in my veins, oh, ooh, _____ the blood __ in my

Pre-Chorus

veins, oh, ooh. _____   But they   nev - er did, ev - er lived, ebb - ing and flow - ing, in -

hib - it - ed, lim - it - ed, till it broke up and it rained down,   it rained __

Chorus

Additional Lyrics

2. Second things second:
   Don't you tell me what you think that I can be.
   I'm the one at the sail, I'm the master of my sea.
   Oh, ooh, the master of my sea. Oh, ooh.

Heathens

from SUICIDE SQUAD

Words and Music by Tyler Joseph

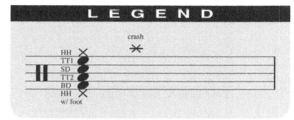

Chorus

All my friends are hea-thens; take it

slow. Wait for them to ask you who you know. Please

don't make an-y sud-den moves. ___ You don't know the half of the a-

buse. ___ All my friends are hea-thens; take it slow. (Watch it.)

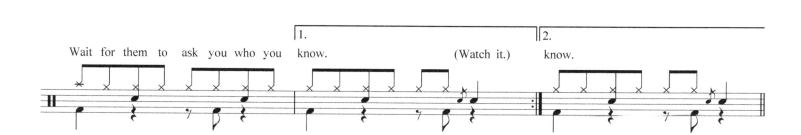

1.	2.

Wait for them to ask you who you know. (Watch it.) know.

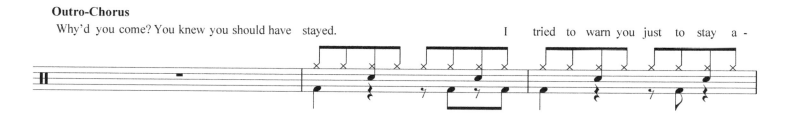

Outro-Chorus

Why'd you come? You knew you should have stayed. I tried to warn you just to stay a-

way. And now they're out-side, read-y to bust. It

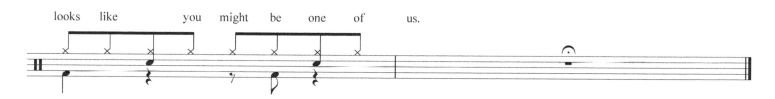

looks like you might be one of us.

Can't Feel My Face

Words and Music by Abel Tesfaye, Max Martin,
Savan Kotecha, Peter Svensson and Ali Payami

Intro
Moderately ♩ = 108

Verse

1. And I know ___ she'll be the death ___ of me, ___ at least ___ ___ we'll both be numb. And she'll al - ways get the best ___ of me, ___ the worst ___ is yet to come. But at least ___ ___ we'll both be beau - ti - ful ___ and stay ___ for - ev - er young. This I know, ___ uh, this I know. ___

Pre-Chorus

___ She told me, "Don't wor - ry a - bout ___ it." She told me, "Don't wor - ry no more." ___ We both know we can't ___ go with - out ___ ___ it. She told me, "You'll nev - er be in love." Oh, oh, woo!

Chorus

I can't feel my face when I'm with you, but I love __ it, but I love __

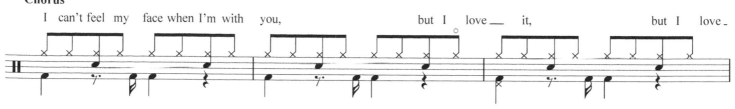

__ it. Oh, ___ I can't feel my face when I'm with you, but I love __

__ it, but I love __ it. **Verse** 2. And I know __ she'll be the death __ of me, __ at least __

__ we'll both be numb. And she'll al - ways get the best __ of me, __ the worst __

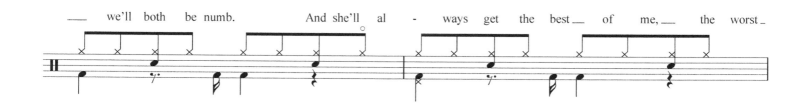

__ is yet to come. All the mis - er - y __ was nec - es - sar - y when __

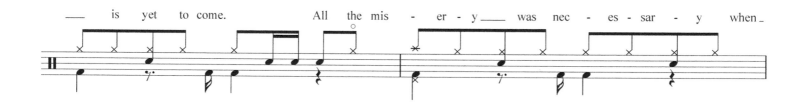

__ we're deep __ in love. __ This I know, __ yeah. Girl, I know. __

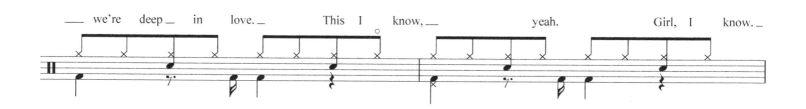

Pre-Chorus

_____ She told me, "Don't wor - ry a - bout __ it." She told me, "Don't

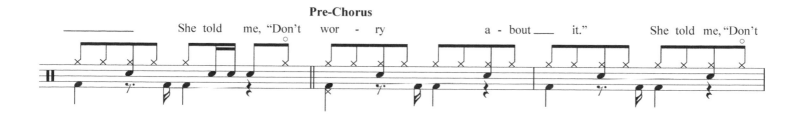

wor - ry   no more." ____   We both   know   we   can't _ go   with - out _

____ it.   She told me, "You'll   nev - er   be   in   love."   Oh,   oh,   woo!

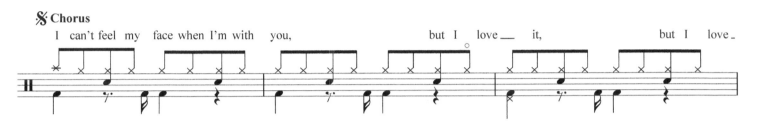

𝄉 **Chorus**

I   can't feel   my   face when   I'm   with   you,   but   I   love _   it,   but   I   love _

____ it.   Oh, ____   I   can't feel   my   face when   I'm   with   you,   but   I   love _

____ it,   but   I   love __ it.   Oh, ____   I   can't feel   my   face when   I'm   with

you,   but   I   love _ it,   but   I   love __ it.   Oh, ____

I   can't feel   my   face when   I'm   with   you,   but   I   love _   it,   but   I   love _

To Coda ⊕

Interlude

— it.   Oh. ____   Ah, _____   ooh. _

_____

Pre-Chorus

She told me, "Don't wor - ry   a - bout _

— it."   She told me, "Don't wor - ry   no more." __   We both know we

can't   go __   with - out ___ it.   She told me, "You'll nev - er __ be in love."

D.S. al Coda

Oh,   oh,   woo!

⊕ **Coda**

Outro

Hey!

15

Human

Words and Music by Jamie Hartman and Rory Graham

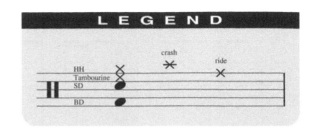

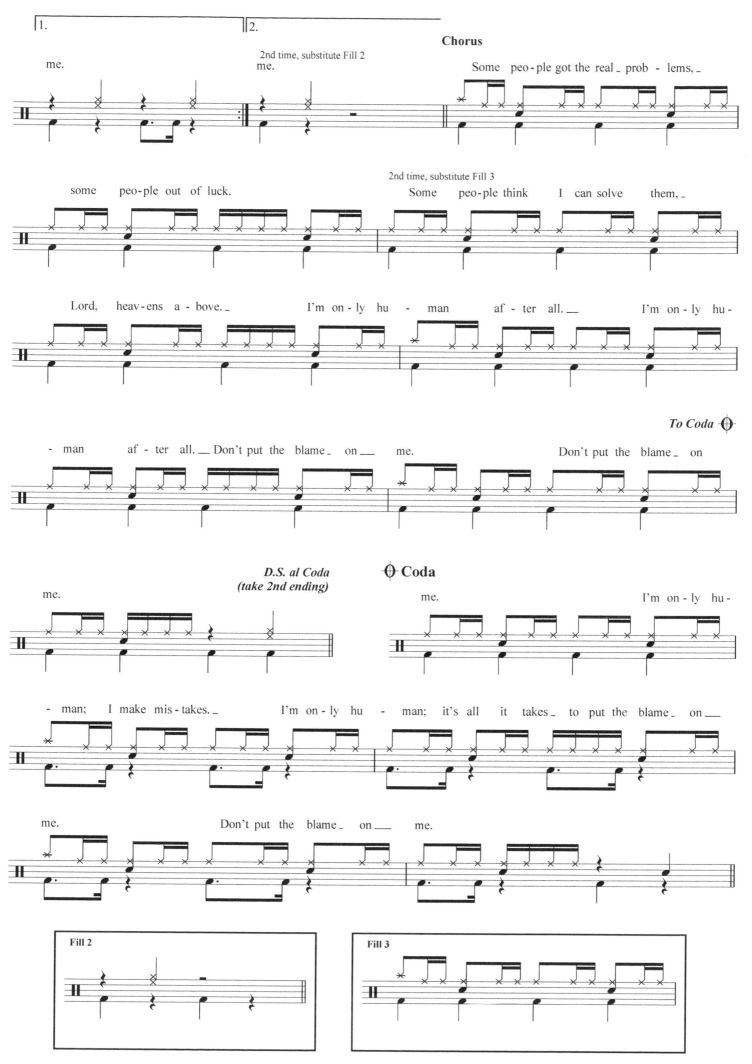

Bridge

Outro

rit.

Additional Lyrics

2. Take a look in the mirror and what do you see?
   Do you see it clearer or are you deceived
   In what you believed?
   'Cause I'm only human after all. You're only human after all.
   Don't put the blame on me. Don't put your blame on me.

3. Don't ask my opinion, don't ask me to lie.
   Then beg for forgiveness for making you cry,
   For making you cry.
   'Cause I'm only human after all. I'm only human after all.
   Don't put your blame on me. Don't put the blame on me.

Lonely Boy

Words and Music by Dan Auerbach, Patrick Carney and Brian Burton

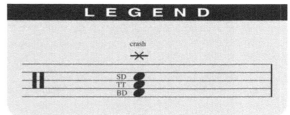

Intro
Moderately fast ♩ = 168

Play 5 times

Play 5 times

Verse

1. Well, I'm so a - bove
2. *See additional lyrics*

___ you, and it's plain to see. ___ But I

came to love ___ you an - y - way. ___

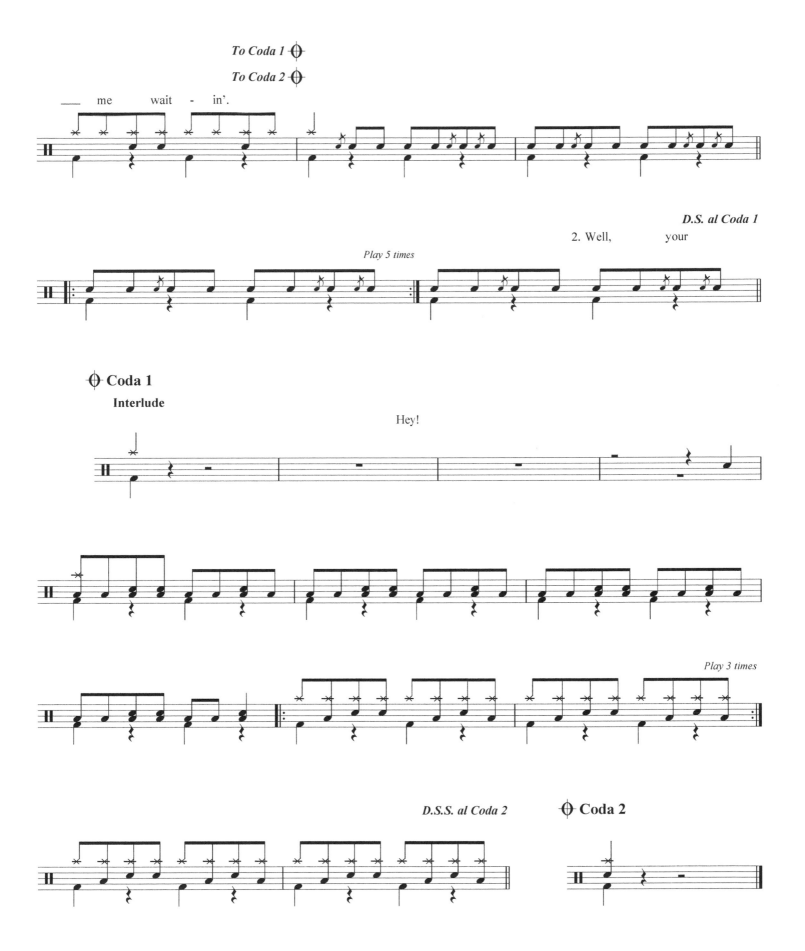

My Songs Know What You Did in the Dark
(Light Em Up)

Words and Music by Andrew Hurley, Joseph Trohman,
Patrick Stump, Peter Wentz, Butch Walker and John Hill

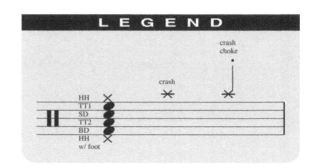

Intro

Moderately fast ♩ = 152

Verse

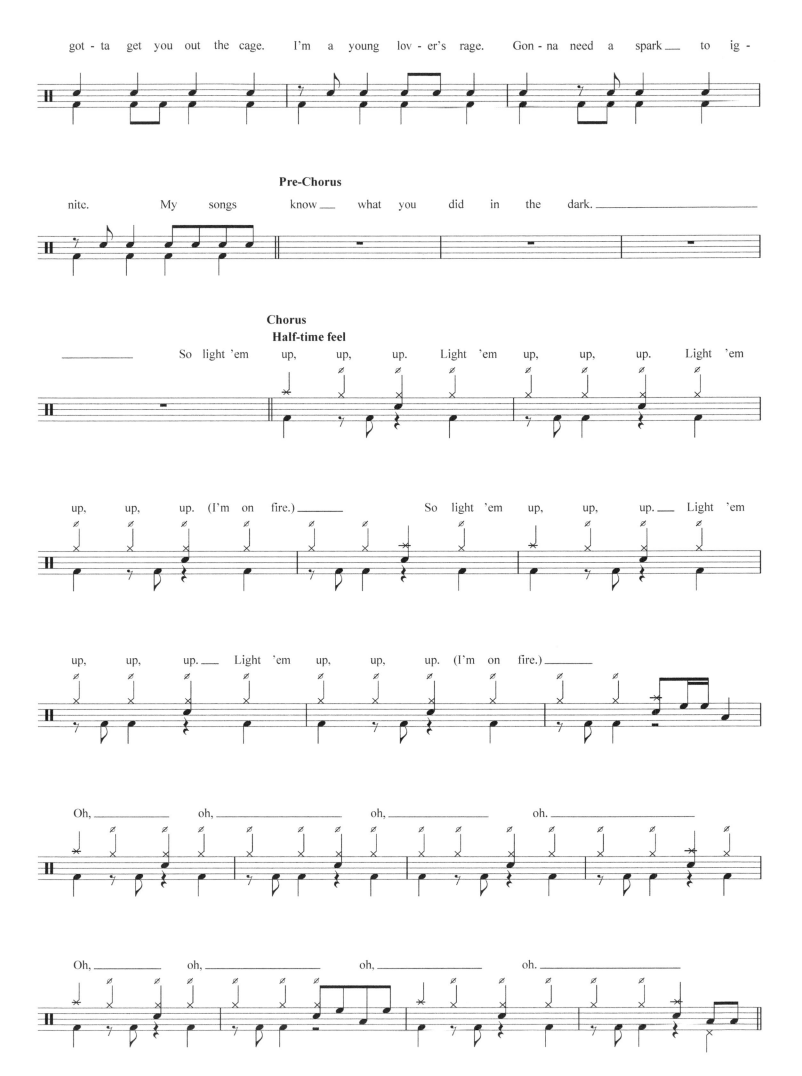

Verse

2. Writ - ers keep writ - ing what they write. Some - where an - oth - er pret - ty vain just

died. I got the scars from to - mor - row, and I wish you could see ___ that you're the

an - ti - dote to ev - 'ry - thing ex - cept for me. A con - stel - la - tion of tears on your

lash - es. Burn ev - 'ry - thing you love then burn the ash - es.

In the end ev - 'ry - thing col - lides. My child - hood spat back out the mon - ster that you

Pre-Chorus

see. My songs know _ what you did in the dark. _____ So light 'em

Chorus

up, up, up. Light 'em up, up, up. Light 'em up, up, up. (I'm on fire.) _

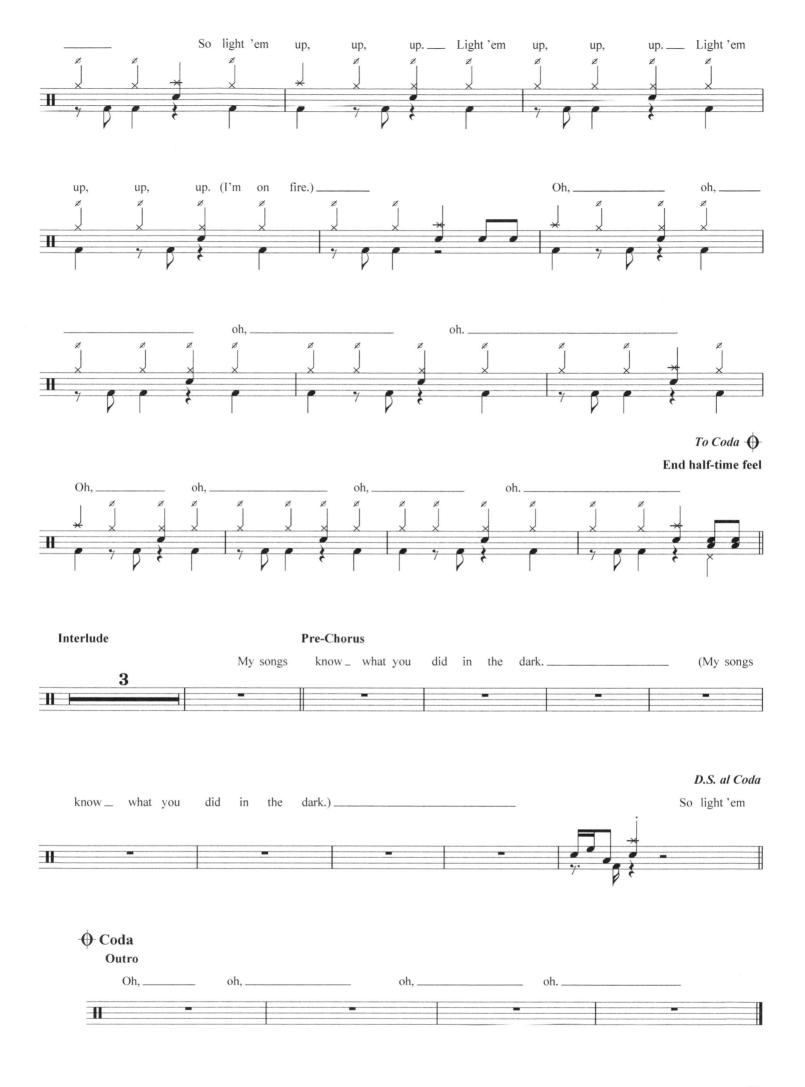

Paradise

Words and Music by Guy Berryman, Jon Buckland,
Will Champion, Chris Martin and Brian Eno

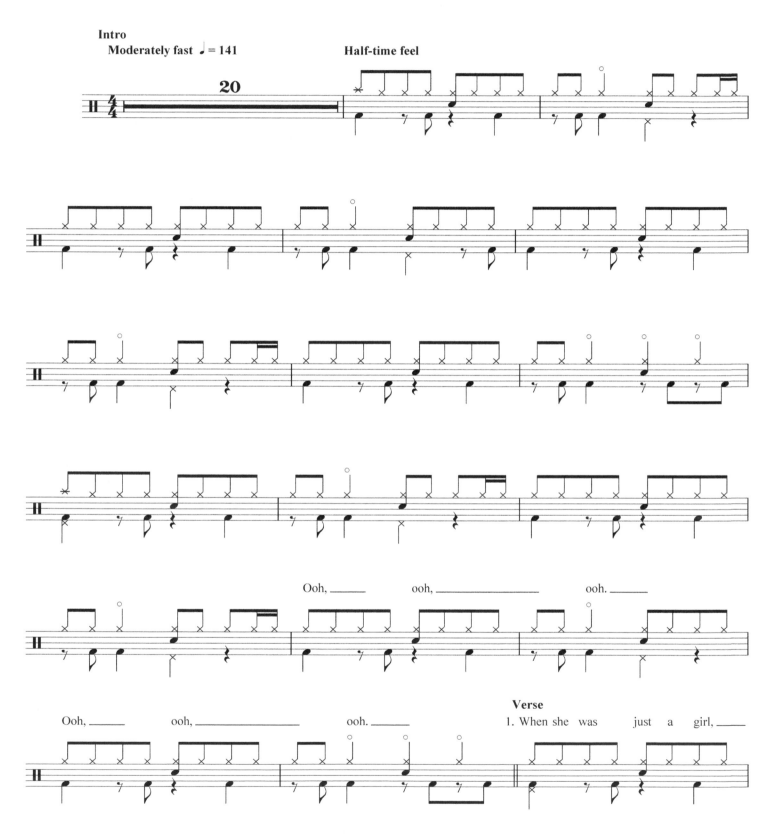

she ex - pect - ed the world, _____ but it

flew a - way from her reach. _____ So she ran a - way in her sleep ___

_____ and dreamed of par - a, par - a, par - a - dise,

par - a, par - a, par - a - dise, par - a, par - a,

par - a - dise, ev - 'ry time she closed ___ her ___ eyes.

Interlude

Ooh, ___ ooh, _____ ooh. ___ Ooh, ___ ooh, _____

3

Verse

___ ooh. ___ 2. When she was just a girl, _____

she ex - pect - ed the world, _____ but it flew a - way from her reach, ___

_____ and the bul - lets catch in her teeth. _____

Life goes on, it gets so heav - y. The wheel ___ breaks the but -

- ter - fly, ev - 'ry tear a wa - ter - fall. In the

night, the storm - y night _____ she'll close her ___ eyes. _____

___ In the night, ___ the storm - y night ___ a - way she'd _

fly. _____

Chorus

And dream of par - a, par - a, _____

la,   la,   la, la, la,   la,   la.   And   so   ly -

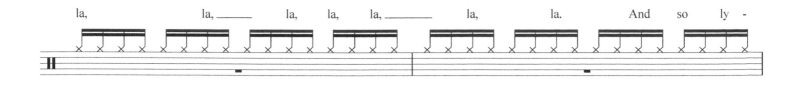

- ing un-der - neath   those storm - y   skies,   she'd say, "Oh, _

_____ oh, ___ I know the   sun must   set   to rise." _   This could be

Chorus

par - a,   par - a, _____ par - a - dise,   par - a,   par - a, _____

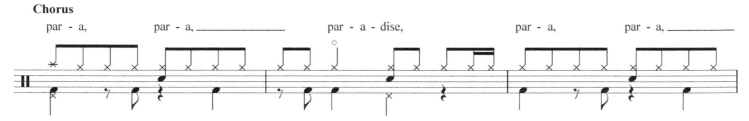

_ par - a - dise. This could be   par - a,   par - a, _____ par - a - dise,

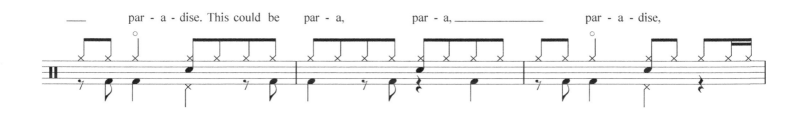

oh, _____ oh. _____ This could be   par - a,   par - a, _____

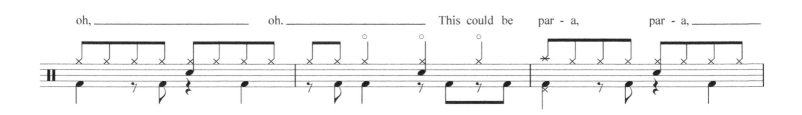

_ par - a - dise,   par - a,   par - a, _____ par - a - dise. Could be

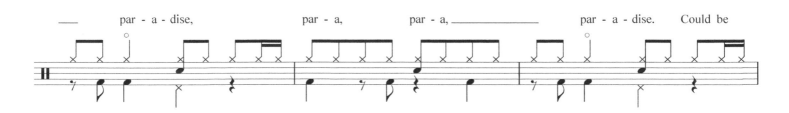

*1st time, vocals tacet.

Outro

rit.

Unsteady

Words and Music by Alexander Junior Grant, Adam Levin,
Casey Harris, Noah Feldshuh and Sam Harris

Intro-Chorus
Half-time feel ♩ = 117

Hold, _____ hold __ on, __ hold __ on __ to me 'cause I'm a

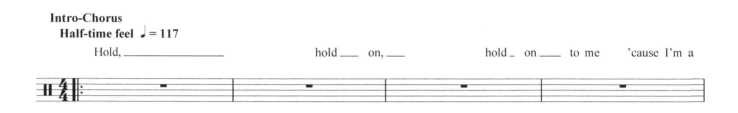

lit-tle un-stead-y, _____ a lit-tle un-stead-y. _____

Interlude

Verse

1. Ma - ma, come here, _____ ap-proach,

ap - pear. _____ Dad - dy, I'm a - lone _____

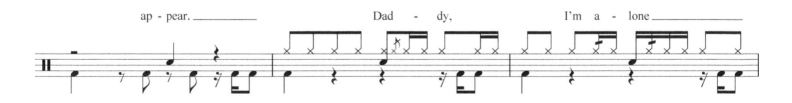

Pre-Chorus

'cause this house don't feel like home. _____ If you love __

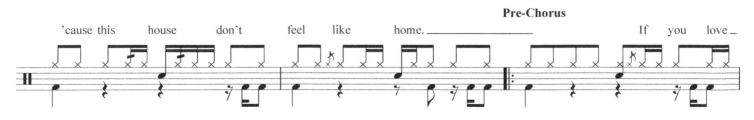

Wish I Knew You

Words and Music by Robert Ingraham, George Gekas, Ed Williams,
Andrew Campanelli, Zachary Feinberg, David Shaw and Michael Girardot

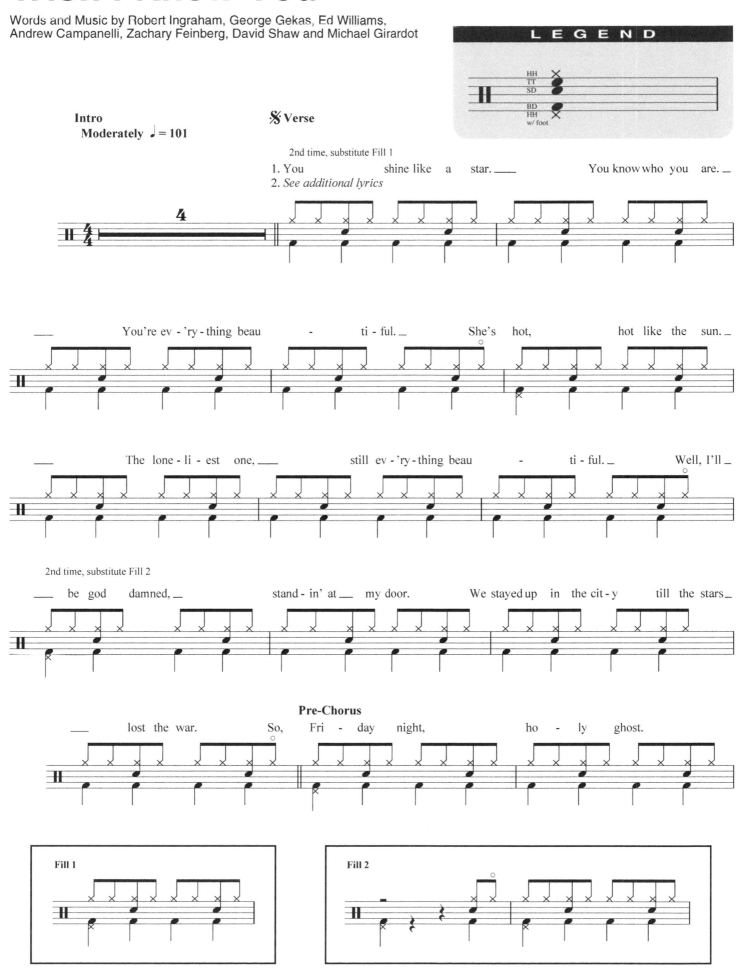

Take me to your lev - el.　　Show me the one ＿ I need the most, ＿＿＿＿　　I need the most. ＿

𝄋 𝄋 Chorus

I wish I knew ＿ you when I was young.　　We could -'ve got ＿ so high. ＿

＿　　Now we're here, ＿ it's been so long.

To Coda 1 ⊕

To Coda 2 ⊕

Two stran - gers in the bright ＿ lights. ＿＿＿＿　　Oh, ＿ and I hope you don't ＿

＿ mind.　　We can share ＿ my mood, ＿＿＿ yeah. ＿＿

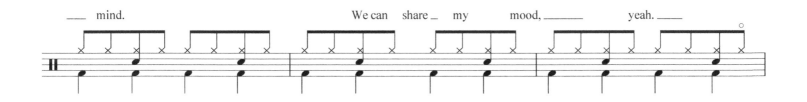

Two stran-gers in the bright ＿ lights.　　I wish I knew ＿ you. ＿＿＿

Fill 3

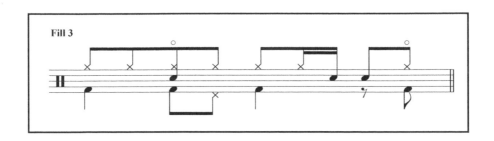

Interlude

I wish I knew _ you.   Oh,   I wish I knew _ you when I was   young.

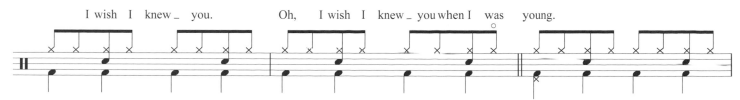

D.S. al Coda 1

⊕ Coda 1

_ lights. _____   Oh, _ and I hope you don't _ mind.

We can share _ my   mood, _____   yeah. _   Two   stran-gers in the bright _

_ lights.   I wish I knew _ you. _____   I wish I knew _ you.

Oh,   I wish I knew _ you   when I was   young.   **Interlude**

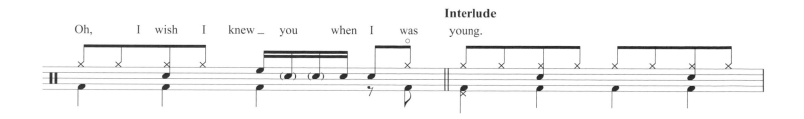

May - be we can share my

Bridge

Additional Lyrics

2. Truth, it's all that you need.
   You bury that seed; it's ev'rything beautiful.
   And that sound comes from the underground.
   It's all inside you now, it's ev'rything beautiful.
   But what you, what you, what you, what you running from?
   And they got, they got, they got, they got you on the run.

HAL•LEONARD®
DRUM PLAY-ALONG

AUDIO ACCESS INCLUDED

The Drum Play-Along™ Series will help you play your favorite songs quickly and easily! Just follow the drum notation, listen to the audio to hear how the drums should sound, and then play-along using the separate backing tracks. The lyrics are also included for reference. The audio files are enhanced so you can adjust the recording to any tempo without changing pitch!

1. Pop/Rock
00699742.................$14.99

2. Classic Rock
00699741.................$16.99

3. Hard Rock
00699743.................$17.99

4. Modern Rock
00699744.................$19.99

5. Funk
00699745.................$16.99

7. Punk Rock
00699747.................$14.99

8. '80s Rock
00699832.................$16.99

9. Cover Band Hits
00211599.................$16.99

10. blink-182
00699834.................$19.99

11. Jimi Hendrix Experience: Smash Hits
00699835.................$19.99

12. The Police
00700268.................$16.99

13. Steely Dan
00700202.................$17.99

15. The Beatles
00256656.................$17.99

16. Blues
00700272.................$17.99

17. Nirvana
00700273.................$16.99

18. Motown
00700274.................$16.99

19. Rock Band: Modern Rock Edition
00700707.................$17.99

21. Weezer
00700959.................$14.99

22. Black Sabbath
00701190.................$17.99

23. The Who
00701191.................$22.99

24. Pink Floyd – Dark Side of the Moon
00701612.................$19.99

25. Bob Marley
00701703.................$19.99

26. Aerosmith
00701887.................$19.99

27. Modern Worship
00701921.................$19.99

29. Queen
00702389.................$17.99

30. Dream Theater
00111942.................$24.99

31. Red Hot Chili Peppers
00702992.................$19.99

32. Songs for Beginners
00704204.................$15.99

33. James Brown
00117422.................$17.99

34. U2
00124470.................$19.99

35. Buddy Rich
00124640.................$19.99

36. Wipe Out & 7 Other Fun Songs
00125341.................$19.99

37. Slayer
00139861.................$17.99

38. Eagles
00143920.................$17.99

39. Kiss
00143937.................$16.99

40. Stevie Ray Vaughan
00146155.................$16.99

41. Rock Songs for Kids
00148113.................$15.99

42. Easy Rock Songs
00148143.................$15.99

45. Bon Jovi
00200891.................$17.99

46. Mötley Crüe
00200892.................$16.99

47. Metallica: 1983-1988
00234340.................$19.99

48. Metallica: 1991-2016
00234341.................$19.99

49. Top Rock Hits
00256655.................$16.99

51. Deep Purple
00278400.................$16.99

52. More Songs for Beginners
00278403.................$14.99

53. Pop Songs for Kids
00298650.................$15.99

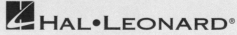

HAL•LEONARD®

Visit Hal Leonard Online at
www.halleonard.com

Prices, contents and availability subject to change without notice and may vary outside the US.

DRUM TRANSCRIPTIONS
FROM HAL LEONARD

THE BEATLES DRUM COLLECTION

26 drum transcriptions of some of the Beatles' best, including: Back in the U.S.S.R. • Birthday • Can't Buy Me Love • Eight Days a Week • Help! • Helter Skelter • I Saw Her Standing There • Ob-La-Di, Ob-La-Da • Paperback Writer • Revolution • Sgt. Pepper's Lonely Hearts Club Band • Something • Twist and Shout • and more.

00690402 . . . .$19.99

BEST OF BLINK-182

Features Travis Barker's bashing beats from a baker's dozen of Blink's best. Songs: Adam's Song • Aliens Exist • All the Small Things • Anthem Part II • Dammit • Don't Leave Me • Dumpweed • First Date • Josie • Pathetic • The Rock Show • Stay Together for the Kids • What's My Age Again?

00690621 . . . .$22.99

DRUM CHART HITS

Authentic drum transcriptions of 30 pop and rock hits are including: Can't Stop the Feeling • Ex's & Oh's • Get Lucky • Moves like Jagger • Shake It Off • Thinking Out Loud • 24K Magic • Uptown Funk • and more.

00234062 . . . .$17.99

INCUBUS DRUM COLLECTION

Drum transcriptions for 13 of the biggest hits from this alt-metal band. Includes: Are You In? • Blood on the Ground • Circles • A Crow Left of the Murder • Drive • Megalomaniac • Nice to Know You • Pardon Me • Privilege • Stellar • Talk Shows on Mute • Wish You Were Here • Zee Deveel.

00690763 . . . .$17.95

BEST OF THE DAVE MATTHEWS BAND FOR DRUMS

Cherry Lane Music

Note-for-note transcriptions of Carter Beauford's great drum work: The Best of What's Around • Crash into Me • What Would You Say.

02500184 . . . .$19.95

DAVE MATTHEWS BAND – FAN FAVORITES FOR DRUMS

Cherry Lane Music

Exact drum transcriptions of every Carter Beauford beat from 10 of the most requested DMB hits: Crush • Dancing Nancies • Everyday • Grey Street • Jimi Thing • The Space Between • Tripping Billies • Two Step • Warehouse • Where Are You Going.

02500643 . . . .$19.95

METALLICA – ...AND JUSTICE FOR ALL

Cherry Lane Music

Drum transcriptions to every song from Metallica's blockbuster album, plus complete drum setup diagrams, and background notes on Lars Ulrich's drumming style.

02503504 . . . .$19.99

METALLICA – BLACK

Cherry Lane Music

Matching folio to their critically acclaimed self-titled album. Includes: Enter Sandman * Sad But True * The Unforgiven * Don't Tread On Me * Of Wolf And Man * The God That Failed * Nothing Else Matters * and 5 more metal crunchers.

02503509 . . . .$22.99

METALLICA – MASTER OF PUPPETS

Cherry Lane Music

Matching folio to the best-selling album. Includes: Master Of Puppets • Battery • Leper Messiah • plus photos.

02503502 . . . .$19.99

METALLICA – RIDE THE LIGHTNING

Cherry Lane Music

Matching folio to Metallica's second album, including: Creeping Death • Fade To Black • and more.

02503507 . . . .$19.99

NIRVANA DRUM COLLECTION

Features transcriptions of Dave Grohl's actual drum tracks on 17 hits culled from four albums: *Bleach, Nevermind, Incesticide* and *In Utero*. Includes the songs: About a Girl • All Apologies • Blew • Come as You Are • Dumb • Heart Shaped Box • In Bloom • Lithium • (New Wave) Polly • Smells like Teen Spirit • and more. Also includes a drum notation legend.

00690316 . . . .$22.99

BEST OF RED HOT CHILI PEPPERS FOR DRUMS

Note-for-note drum transcriptions for every funky beat blasted by Chad Smith on 20 hits from *Mother's Milk* through *By the Way*! Includes: Aeroplane • Breaking the Girl • By the Way • Californication • Give It Away • Higher Ground • Knock Me Down • Me and My Friends • My Friends • Right on Time • Scar Tissue • Throw Away Your Television • True Men Don't Kill Coyotes • Under the Bridge • and more.

00690587 . . . .$24.99

RED HOT CHILI PEPPERS – GREATEST HITS

Essential for Peppers fans! Features Chad Smith's thunderous drumming transcribed note-for-note from their *Greatest Hits* album. 15 songs: Breaking the Girl • By the Way • Californication • Give It Away • Higher Ground • My Friends • Scar Tissue • Suck My Kiss • Under the Bridge • and more.

00690681 . . . .$22.99

RED HOT CHILI PEPPERS – I'M WITH YOU

Note-for-note drum transcriptions from the group's tenth album: The Adventures of Rain Dance Maggie • Annie Wants a Baby • Brendan's Death Song • Dance, Dance, Dance • Did I Let You Know • Ethiopia • Even You Brutus? • Factory of Faith • Goodbye Hooray • Happiness Loves Company • Look Around • Meet Me at the Corner • Monarchy of Roses • Police Station.

00691168 . . . .$22.99

RUSH – THE SPIRIT OF RADIO: GREATEST HITS 1974-1987

17 exact drum transcriptions from Neil Peart! Includes: Closer to the Heart • Fly by Night • Freewill • Limelight • Red Barchetta • Spirit of Radio • Subdivisions • Time Stand Still • Tom Sawyer • The Trees • Working Man • 2112 (I Overture & II Temples of Syrinx).

00323857 . . . .$22.99

HAL•LEONARD®

7777 W. BLUEMOUND RD. P.O. BOX 13819 MILWAUKEE, WI 53213

www.halleonard.com

0222
154

Prices, contents and availability subject to change without notice.